DOWN
TO THE
BONE

Wild Rising Press &
Poetry Mesa Chapbook Series

Down
TO THE
Bone

POEMS

Amy Wray Irish

EVERGREEN, COLORADO

Book & Cover Design: Mary M. Meade
Illustrations: L_Kramer/via IStock
Editor: Judyth Hill

wildrisingpress.com
ISBN 978-1-957468-08-2—First Edition

For all my wild women,
burning to make things right.

⚮

"Baba Yaga gave Vasilisa a skull with a fire inside
as a guide back through the dark forest, and home."

—from the Russian fairy tale *Vasilisa the Beautiful*

"The phoenix must burn to emerge."

—Janet Fitch, *White Oleander*

Contents

DOWN
TO THE
BONE

Listen

This is the sound of an unheard body straining
at the seams—
the speak-only-when-spoken-to desire,
the tongue numb under icy blood.

This is the sound of the silent taut muscles
as they crack open—
the sudden snap, stitch by stitch,
of lips no longer sewn shut.

This is the sound of a smothered pulse bursting
from the chest—
tired of the hollow dance
without relief, without release.

This is sound of Snow White's heart under glass
shattered—
just one white-hot jolt
restarts the rhythm, recharges the voltage

so her once-frozen bones can explode.

Casting a Bone Broth Spell

The elders are surprised at my ignorance
of how to brew the potion
they drink to conjure life from death.

Taken aback at the way my hands
balk at pulling apart the carcass
to strip skeleton out of flesh.

Stunned by mouth and tongue turned
aside at the taste of three-day soup
which steamed kitchens for generations.

The motherless child, in stories,
is still encircled by women. Rooted (for good
or ill) in stepmother, widow, and witch.

Each added something to the recipe,
offered the girl's cookpot of self
a necessary ingredient to season the stew.

But then the editors stepped in, slapped down
that slippery, many-faced mother. Decreed
only the wicked would cook up a cauldron of bone.

I'll grind your bones to make my bread,
proclaims the giantess. *I'll roast your meat*
and drink the dripping juice, promises Baba Yaga.

How poetic she is, this dark chef inside me,
this hungry self, split and hidden in shadow.
How she smells out the savory bits others deny.

On cold days, I now know how to build the fire
that simmers and pulls the marrow from the Earth.
Offered her bloody breast, I've learned to drink.

The Fabric of the Feminine

after Four Purple Velvet Bathrobes by Beverly Semmes

Option I

We all pine for a queen's plush garb. Entrenched
in decadence, even when domestic.

Stitched for stately silence, only
the best for the royal womb. Weighed down

by miles of heavy fabric. Delicious
suffocation of velvet, sweet and far too rich

against the skin, the lips.
She never said *Let them eat cake.*

Her mouth was far too full
of photogenic moments and mistakes.

Option II

Here, mother shoulders a ratty robe,
shudders as others depart for the day.
She stands frozen, framed in the door,
like the faded pictures she displays.

Like her infamous honeymoon
at the crime-scene-photo lake,
where drowning and waving
blurred and merged from far away.

Option III

Next, the liquid cloth waterfalls, swirls,
gathers in a still, dark pool
thick with fishy, beckoning sirens.

Indigo-skinned housewives,
hair hived as they recline
on a '50s settee, drink in hand.

The velvet alcohol they sip
tints their lips plum,
like cold corpses under ice.

From the depths come their murky
murmuration. Their back-alley
afterlife is full of smiles and waves.

Option IV

Unholy robes claim them, one by one.
You think you will escape, but

there's still a ceremonial cloak
of restraint set aside for you.

If you let the water claim you.
If you accept your fate.

The Secret Knowledge of the Earth

The girl burned her eyes to black searching
in books, in fairy tale worlds,

but when the moon quickened
in the belly of the forest

her senses blossomed, eyes unblinded
to the subtleties of night.

And then it was all dark
knowledge, body knowledge.

Instinct. Hunger.
Need. Desire.

Silent unfurling of wings to hunt
a single beating heart.

Talons deep in oak,
deep in flesh.

Unsettling sleepers with her call,
her haunting midnight question:

Who? Who will join me
in this ritual of sacred meat?

Who? Who will study
our future by the bones within?

The Princess in Disguise

"I shall require a mantle made of a thousand skins of rough fur sewn together."

—*Grimm's Complete Fairy Tales*

When she paints herself a fierce new face,
a grimace of feather and mud and ash—
she is not in hiding.
When she throws away her certainty,
gives up family, fortune, future crown—
she is not incognito.

When she packs away her skin,
labors instead under the rough,
heavy layer of the recently slain—
she is not in disguise.

She has finally stopped
donning the costume, covering up
her ugly, wearing her skin inside out.
She has released that caged creature
trained in polite language, pleasant laugh.
She has thrown away those pearls,
that string of sedatives
with the bite of new-cut teeth. You see,

When she climbs into the rotten center
of the gnarled and deadened wood,
the living tree long-gone,
she gets along just fine without the light.

It is you, dear reader—
a child still so tenderly penned up
in the princess prison—
who is finally
facing the dark.

The Bloody Show

It's quite a pantomime. A modern
Punch and Judy. Just watch
as the curtains open, red velvet parted
to reveal the theater of operation.
Come meet the dramatis personae—

A clowning doctor who pokes
and prods, trips, drops his tools;
and the stirruped Judy (mostly legs)
who has quite the kick, refusing
to let Punch near her jumpy belly.

Behold as hijinks ensue! A Lamaze book
brains the doctor; an IV drip is wielded
like a lasso, a whip. Back and forth,
slap and stick, until a needle
of comic proportions is produced.

The Doc injects Pitocin to induce
and make the lady behave.
A few sound effects set the mood
for the magic of childbirth
(a donkey's bray, a yowling cat).

The audience howls with laughter
when the Doc is doused in fake blood.
At last, the baby ejects the capsule,
a tiny human cannonball, barely caught.
The Doc fumbles the bundle (part played

by a hot potato) while other puppets
take the unfit mother away. The audience
claps, throws coins. Every Punch
in the world cheers, gives his own wife
a sinister glare. Calls for the puppeteer

to pull the strings, pick up the stick again.

Lipstick

Scarlet as an ibis
    with a broken neck

"We'll update your look,
    a pop of color" —they promise

Meaning I'm monochrome
    face   a faded painting

So I let them operate
    their machinery

Apply the fake mouth
    the flare gun

Become the storefront
    mannequin

The glossy mating display
    exotic   as hibiscus

I am crafted
    in plastic

Ripe, tempting
    tasty   as paste

My artificial lips firmly attached
    I'm declared a success

Now I'm perfect
   a real doll

Lips sticky
   stuck.

The Crushes

a haibun

Instead of swept off my feet I wanted to be knocked down, dizzied by the concussive blast. *Need me with as much force,* I cried out. *Crash into me like train wreck.* Every full-body impact of desire hit with tectonic savagery, shaking me with the aftershocks. I don't know why I wanted so fiercely, only that without that feeling I was left with crushing absence, a hunger I could not fill. A bird without its grinding stone, starving to death. So I craved the weight, the blow like a brick to my temporal lobe. I wanted to be fully crushed in the vise of the body, with no mind left to debate. I didn't know how violent those blows would get, how many times they would scar.

Now I put down stones
for each self I gave away
and lay a new path.

Bluebeard's Promises

*"Here are the house keys," he told his bride. "You may go
everywhere and look at everything, except for the closet that this
little key unlocks."*

—*Grimm's Complete Fairy Tales*

I'll Live Ever After

happily, he swears—if I twine the rope, tie back
my own hands. Stay blank as a storybook

for him to write. Await the touch
of his pen, to bear his issue in ink.

And then he offers a key. Leaves me
to consider: am I this empty

castle, rooms vacant until he returns?
I have keys to all the doors. I may go—

Anywhere. Everywhere. (Nowhere.)

I'll Awaken with a Kiss

after just a hundred years—if I hold the apple
without a single want, obediently sleepwalk

the halls of hunger. Instead, the key
is continually at hand, fingers unable to deny

or hide what I crave. My thumb stroking
the metal, pricked by the insistent teeth

that bite open the flesh of self.

I'll Have Everything I Want

as long as it's gowns, parties, guests—if I don't ask
about my missing sisters. If I accept

my anesthesia, my continual distraction. Instead
I wield the key like a sword, ready to strip away

the skin, to look beyond the bones crossed
in warning. Ready for the revelation

of my own inner workings.

I Can Save Them All

with my sewing and sweetness—if I force down
silence as my daily meal, pick the roughest fibers

and bleed into all I weave. Don't I want
to work hard, bow my head, take my blows?

No. Instead, I'll break down the door
of the locked-up past. I'll rip aside delusion,

open my eyes to all the bodies. I'll stop letting it go
unspoken. Soon, I'll see these splintered women

as parts of myself I need to be whole. Soon
I'll choose to consume the forbidden fruit

straight through to the pulsing core.

The Owl Delivers Her Pellet

"I raise up my voice—not so that I can shout, but so that those without a voice can be heard."

—*Malala Yousafzai*

I am described as silent—
credited as watchful, quiet.
But in my cage I have choked
back so much, my throat
clogged with such rotten meals.

Quick, quick down the gullet
goes everything I am told
to swallow. But I don't
just accept what I'm given.
I dissolve the dead

meat of every message
down to the bone,
and I compose a little
bundle of my own
I return to sender.

All the complexity digested,
the mess stripped out,
the fat burned down for fuel,
the story rendered clean
and stark and white.

Still, I make no sound
while I deconstruct, decaying
the unnecessary away.
When I open my beak
I do not speak. Not yet.

I wait until a tight-woven web
of their splintered words
can be laid out at their feet.
Heaving and retching
I feel them coming, finally,

and sing as I spit them out.

The Moon of Fire

cenote—a natural pit or sinkhole that exposes groundwater. In the Yucatán Peninsula of Mexico, cenotes were commonly water supplies for the ancient Maya and sites for sacrificial offerings.

Burning like a fiery opal, like molten
gold uncooled in the ocean
of the sky, the moon's gleam
lights the liquid of the sacrificial pool.

Those *cenote* waters drip flame
all the way down. The seductive moon
sparks like flint on the treasure waiting,
winking and blazing in invitation.

The dive looks so easy, the depths
so safe. But when *el fuego*
de la luna ignites an urge
to plunge in, you have a choice—

To be another sacrifice, swallowed
and stilled with so many others;
or to drink from the pool of the moon
yourself and be filled with its seed—

The power of its ancient light,
its burning blood.

When the Rage Returns

You wake with the great weight of it
alighting, the pierce of its talons
gripping the throbbing ridge of your brow.

You are risen but cannot rise, are not allowed
as it lifts and shifts its legs—
pricking temple, neck nerve, jawline.

The bridge of your nose, arch
of your cheekbones, ache
as it crosses you, explores its former territory.

How long until it finds purchase, settles
and roosts? Predatory breath
stirs your hair, weaves a tangled nest.

How it presses you down
into motionless mountain, obedient
arbor, limbs aching to be limber

Again. But only stiff and still
can you silence it, stop its feathers
from ruffling, from rustling, stop

Its claws from constantly razoring
deeper in. If you are wooden, leaden,
stone, it will cease its clutch and shrieking

Cry. You will feel nothing
again. Or you could let this bird
of prey—

       your anger

              —in.

Believing in Magic

I do not believe in magic
when the body displayed in spotlight
splits.

       To be a woman is to be
on stage. To be cut. Publicly
broken by degrees
with such fanfare and flourish
that the schism inside

          the box spreads
completely, words from deeds, head
from sex.

         We are the spectacle
that elevates, a tribute to a greatness
outside ourselves.

         No, the magic
doesn't come until the return, when two
rent parts stand before us

          flushed with rebirth.
Because

       I've been there, summoned
to this service, pressed into the mold

          of sacrifice,
convinced I volunteered.

Because

         we've all been there, feeling
the damp of our insides

            trickling down
beneath the cover-up, the perfectly

    corrected clothes,
still wet from the serrated edge of skin
that isn't quite sewn up.

        Now. Now I get religion.

Because maybe this girl—this body,
this piece of the bloody congregation—
is finally blessed. Maybe she's the one
made whole, and all the rest of us
were the dress rehearsal, the practice
or the price

        to make the magic real.

Rewriting the Mythology

We all begin the same—

Saints and sorcerers and monster-slayers. All of us saviors.
Seen on every page, spun again and again in narratives of the
daring, fables of the fair. But eventually, real-life complexities
crack us open. Our chronicles of self are broken at the spine.
And we turn to a different story, a different shelf. Perhaps

because we can't stand the senseless sweat of sewing nettles
(turns out it's all sacrifice and silence). Perhaps because we'd
rather wildly cry, become a brother swan. Perhaps because our
hearts hurt—not for beanstalk Jack— but for the harp, sick
of playing on demand. Perhaps because we're disinclined to
wonder about the getting of wishes, and more interested in
getting the fair folk in bed. Perhaps

because we've seen those former heroes on the street, their
slack faces empty of any meaning. They wait, nameless grains
of sand sleeping on the beach of the masses, all waiting to be
called to story, to become. And we are the few who refuse to
huddle on the endless, rocky shore and wait through book
after book until some Thor calls up a lightning bolt to shock us
awake and make us act. Perhaps

because we are the few, the very few, who dare to rise up in
a sandstorm whirl and harness the electric power of creation
ourselves, wielding the written lightning to strike the beach
and forge the melting sand to glass—

and start a mythology all our own.

Let Us Begin

"It's spring ... and the just unfurling leaves are full of infant chlorophyll."

—*Tony Hoagland*

As spring cracks open—all downy and wet,
with eyes squinted into the dawn—
                Let us begin
to be new ourselves. All body-slick
and wonderment. Let us begin
with that first hypnotism of sky, that first delight
of description in our mouths,
that first color of spring so verdant that
its vibrance escapes every word's confinement
and is only expressed by our breath
opening as we sing
this throat-pulsing, succulent-noted song.
                Let us begin
a new calendar filled only with new days,
every day the equinox, every day
a seed's crackling earthquake birth.
                Let us begin
despite those who drag us back, making plans
and demands. Despite those who upend the earth,
who deny and try to forget the trees
making love all around us.
                Let us begin
to reconcile with the earth. Let us begin to believe

we can. Let us begin to remember that we are
the process too, part of the endless shattering
of snow cover, driven apart by the piercing crest
of the infant white crocus as it crowns. Yes.

Let us begin

like the earth, always a new bloom bursting
at the starting line, aching to open
and let sun in.

The Angels Underground

When I planted my heart-
shaped spade into the earth,
began digging in her rain-fresh
wonder, I plunged fathoms down.

Deep into her memory
I dove, through history's permafrost.
As I turned over the decades, seeking soil
to turn my darkness into growth

She revealed the great, sainted grandmother
of all earthworms. Fat as my thumb
and sinuous as a gliding garden snake,
but never mistaken for that messenger

of forked roads. This seraph curled
instinctively back to ground, its true north,
rapturously pointing out the direction
where all my fresh starts belong.

Perhaps you have seen greater.
Perhaps you have even communed
with a whole underground host.
But in my decades of fruitless digging

for a land to plant my pitted heart,
this angel of the earth was my first—
an indication at last
I'm putting down roots.

Speaking Serpent

When I approach the shadows
she pauses her slim, slate form.

Doubles back and flickers the black fork
of her tongue to double check

if it's safe to talk. She cannot speak,
of course, but even in silence

communicates much with the coil
and calligraphy of her body.

With mine, I move in supplication,
dance the words to my dangerous ask.

In response, she swims through the grass,
asking *Where*? and *When*?

with every curve. Scales a shimmer
of her Morse code message.

My hands flutter the answer: *Here*
and *Now*. At this she stiffens, darts swift

as an arrow. Points the way
to escape Eden.

And is forever branded
a dark serpent

of questionable intent

rather than one sister

showing another

how to shed her useless skin.

The Barbie Conspiracy

after the Barbie poems by Denise Duhamel

The luckiest of Ken dolls wakes to find
he's shacking up with beautiful twins.
It's every frat boy's dream!
Sandwiched every night
between four silicone breasts
which will never age, never sag.
The Dream House lives up to its name.

But why are they both named Barbie?
There's nothing to separate them,
no differences of taste or flaws.
Shouldn't one prefer drinks at the beach, the other
a drive in the Barbie convertible?
They do everything with him
together, both blonde, perky,
and forever frozen in smile.

He starts to wonder, are they really sisters?
He ponders until that fateful day
of illumination—a third arrives.
It's more bodies than his two hands
can handle. These multiple Barbies swarm
each other in giddy greeting,
identically coiffed and dressed, until
the new one is spun and lost
like the ball in a blonde shell game.

Ken's plastic blood runs cold.

At last, he realizes this is not three
but one unified front. A single
Barbie mind, a Barbie ecosystem
cloned and shipped around the world
with Ken an unnecessary afterthought.
Instead of enjoying the babes
always at his sides, now he shudders.

He worries they're keeping watch.
Like before, there are always two.
But now he can't help but fear
what that third Barbie is doing.
The others never say,
just smile and smile.

The Crime of the Poem

"I am a witness to the crime of the poem."

—*Douglas Kearney*

The poem stormed your defenses
in an angry mob of words.
The poem slipped into your dark
and planted its sleeping seed.

Invited into your home, the poem played
with matches.
Invited to your table, the poem devoured
the flowers.

The poem lurched against you in the subway,
picking your pockets.
The poem pressed against you for a moment,
leaving you aching.

Languorously stretching out its suggestive lines,
the poem sold itself to be undressed.
Brutally kidnapping a body of language,
the poem strip-searched history.

Searching for hidden pockets of decay
to expose, to diagnose, the poem
turned you—turned us all—into bystanders
of this dissection.

And the crime of the poem
came when it made us choose
to be voyeurs complicit in the violation,
or archivists delicately digging in the dark.

Acknowledgments

"The Secret Knowledge of the Earth" was first published in *Waving Hands Review*, Volume 13, 2021.

"The Fabric of the Feminine" was first published online in *Bristlecone*, April 2022.

"Lipstick" was first published in *Ink to Paper,* Volume 6, 2021.

"Rewriting the Mythology" was first published in *Re: (Magpies Anthology*, Vol. 2), 2022.

"The Angels Underground" was first published in *Jasper's Folly*, 2023.

"Speaking Serpent" was first published in *Cadence*, Volume 38, 2020.

"The Barbie Conspiracy" was first published in *Cadence*, Volume 40, 2022.

"The Crime of the Poem" was first published online in *Bristlecone*, April 2022.

About the Author

Amy Wray Irish grew up in Oak Park, Illinois (home to Frank Lloyd Wright and Ernest Hemingway). Raised on regular visits to The Art Institute of Chicago, she developed a passion for writing about art and history. Irish received her MFA from the University of Notre Dame and now lives in the foothills of Colorado with her family. Irish has been published in numerous literary journals and three chapbooks. Her 2021 chapbook, *Breathing Fire*, received the Fledge Award from Middle Creek Publishing. To read more by Amy Wray Irish, go to www.amywrayirish.com.

Gratitude

I would like to extend an enormous thank you to Judyth Hill and Catherine Marenghi of Poetry Mesa for midwifing these poems; to Mary Meade for the artistry of the book's creation; and to Kathleen Willard and Julianza Shavin for both their initial editing and their loving support. I have ongoing gratitude for the Colorado poetry scene—including Marissa Forbes at 20BellowsLit, David Anthony Martin at Middle Creek Publishing, Julie Cummings at Columbine Poets, Brice Maiurro at South Broadway Press, and Sandra S. McRae at *Bristlecone*. And thank you as always to my family. You continue to inspire me with your love.

Selecting a font is the book designer's opportunity to translate the essential qualities of the book into a sensual, visual expression of those qualities. Turning pages, the reader is offered subliminal signals in the font's angles, curves, lines, and "kicks" that resonate with the author's work. Here the designer chose Chaparral Pro for the titles and Adobe Devanagari for the body text. The light, delicate shapes in these fonts form the very bones of these poems. Subtle and lively, Chaparral Pro is the work of noted type designer Carol Twombly. It combines the legibility of the traditional fonts of the 19th century with the grace of 16th-century book lettering: a font whose graceful, precise beauty, suggestive of handwritten letters, invites us into the poems. Adobe Devanagari's origins are enigmatic; designed primarily by Fiona Ross, an expert in Sanskrit, ancient writing systems and Arabic and Indian scripts – the timeline of those systems coincide with translations of the Fairy Tales themselves.